The Mario

Katacha Díaz

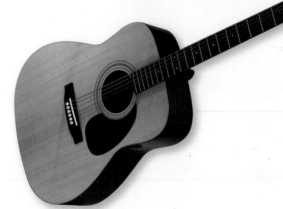

Harcourt Achieve

Rigby • Saxon • Steck-Vaughn

www.HarcourtAchieve.com
1.800.531.5015

I see a boot.

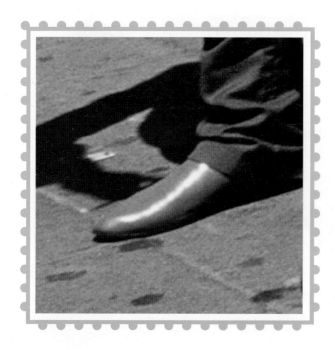

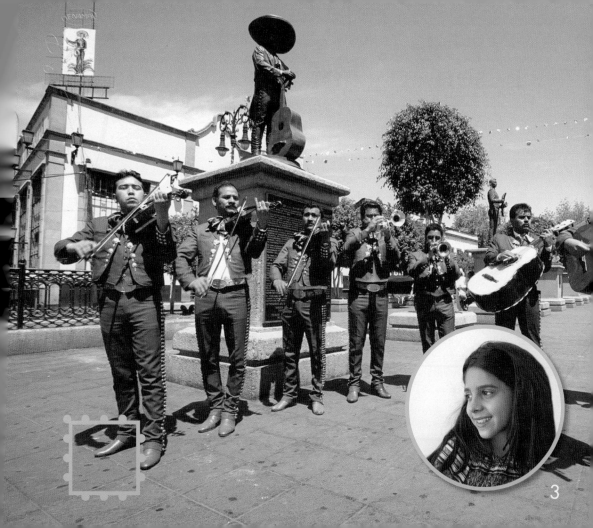

3

I see a hat.

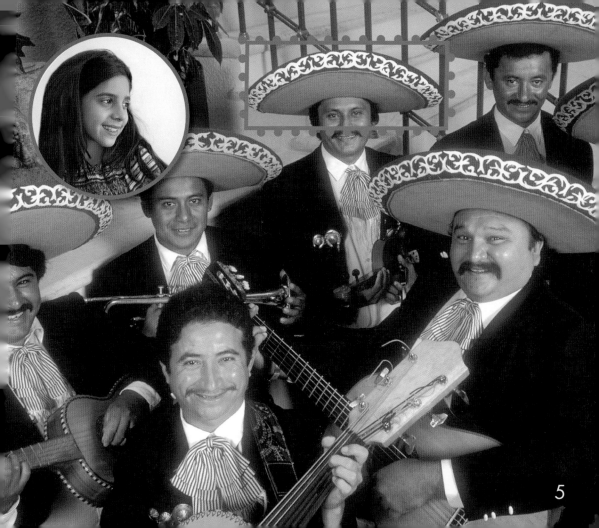

I see a guitar.

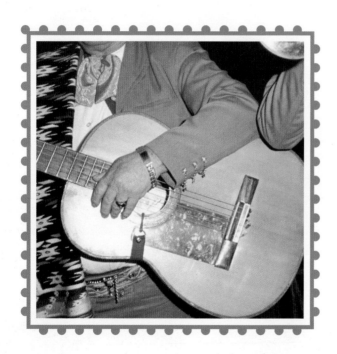

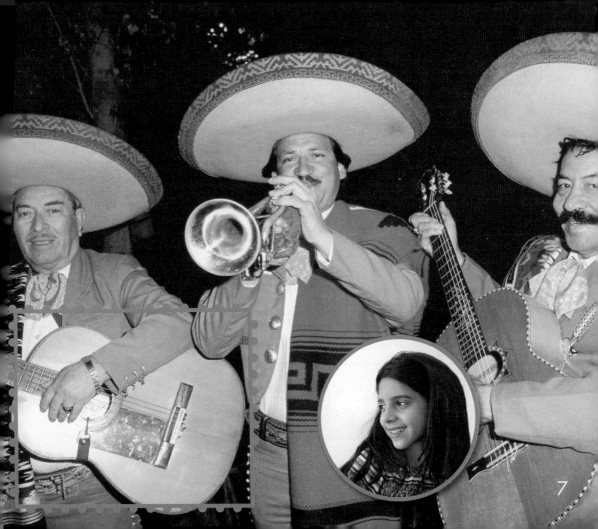

I see a trumpet.

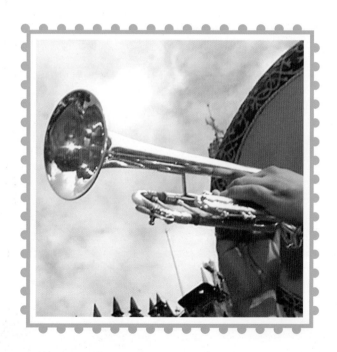

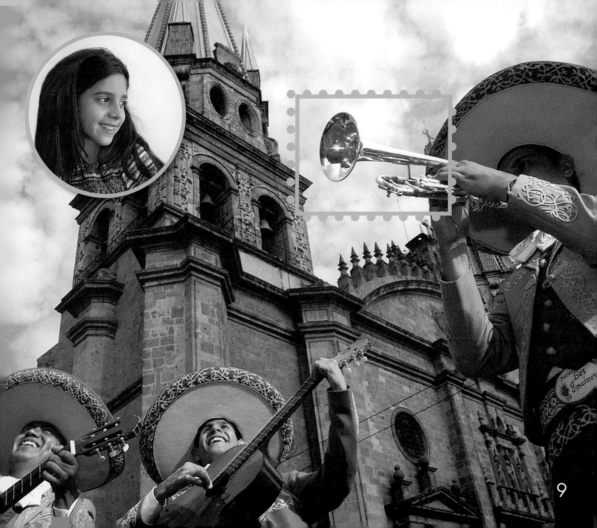

I see a jacket.

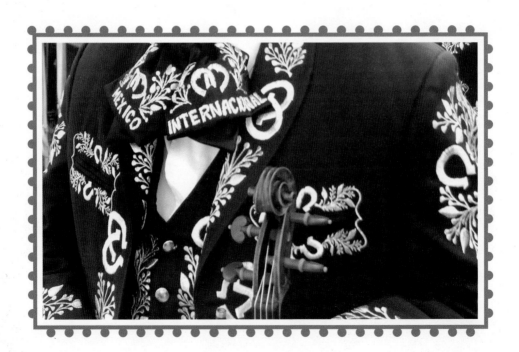

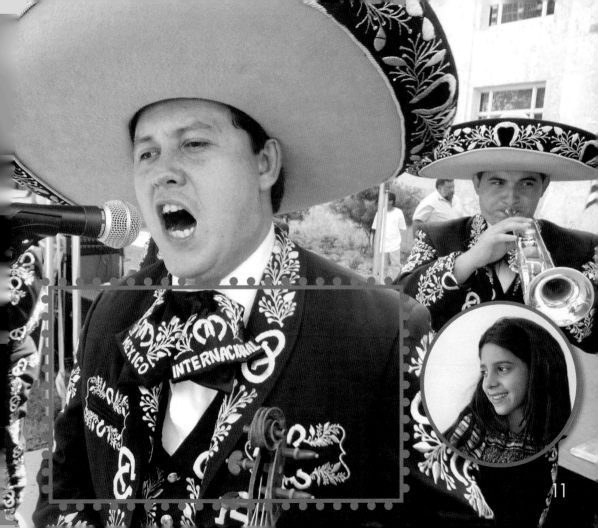

I see a tie.

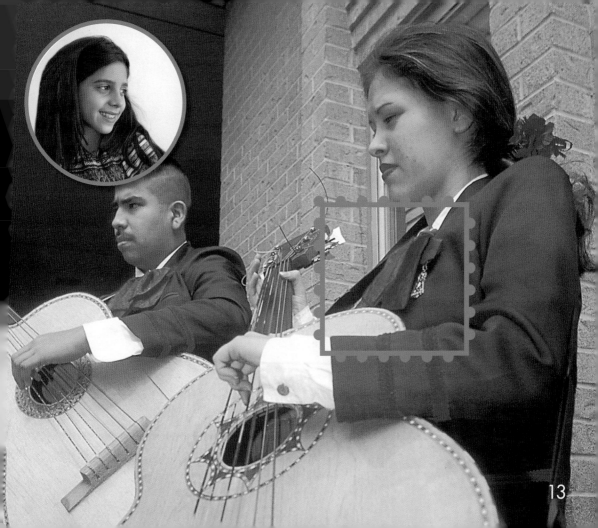

I see a belt.

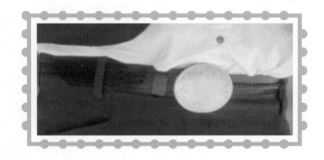

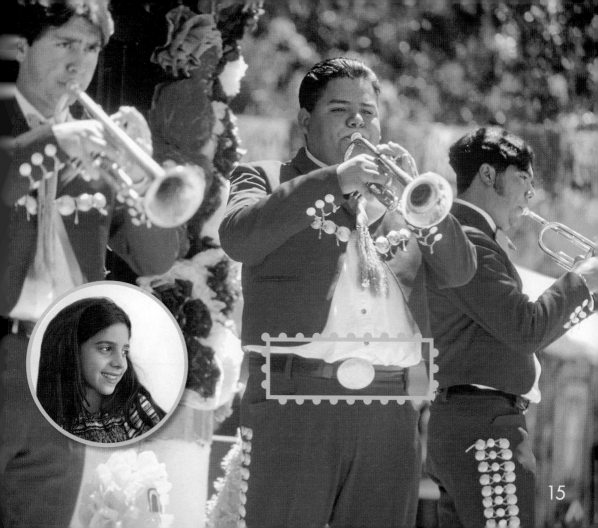

I see a band.

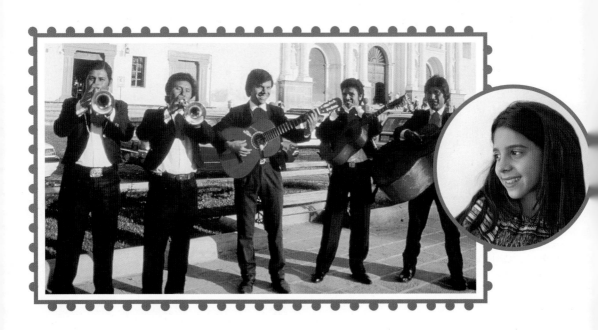